AF131447

BOOK ANALYSIS

By Hudson Cleveland

Gone Girl
BY GILLIAN FLYNN

ANALYSIS 41

FURTHER REFLECTION 49

FURTHER READING 55

GILLIAN FLYNN

AMERICAN AUTHOR

- **Born in Kansas City, Missouri in 1971.**
- **Notable works:**
  - *Sharp Objects* (2006), novel
  - *Dark Places* (2009), novel

Gillian Flynn began her writing career at *U.S. News & World Report* and then *Entertainment Weekly* as a journalist before losing her job at the latter in 2008. Since then, she has focused on fiction, with her novels *Dark Places* and *Gone Girl* being published in 2009 and 2012, respectively, and garnering scattered television and film credits in between and afterward.

Her novels have brought a traditionally overlooked archetype into the limelight: the female villain, particularly of the diabolical and sociopathic sort. Considering the conventional female role is one of reliance on male leads (although in more recent years many writers have also made a conscious effort to challenge this trend by creating complex and independent, but nonetheless 'good', female characters), Flynn's writing poses an interesting counterpoint. That is, no one really expects female characters to inhabit a truly, unapologetically villainous role – in this respect, Flynn writes against the grain of the many mystery writers before her.

GONE GIRL

NICK DUNNE'S WIFE DISAPPEARS, AND ALL THE EVIDENCE POINTS IN HIS DIRECTION

- **Genre:** novel
- **Reference edition:** Flynn, G. (2014) *Gone Girl*. New York City: Broadway Books.
- **1st edition:** 2012
- **Themes:** infidelity, mystery, family, psychology, society of the spectacle, manipulation

On the morning of Nick Dunne's fifth wedding anniversary, his wife, Amy, disappears, leaving behind only signs of a struggle. Initially his small town of Carthage, Missouri, is on his side, but his reactions to the event strike many as odd and off-putting. As investigators gather evidence, everything seems to point toward Nick – from a lack of an alibi, to exorbitant credit card expenditures, to an increased life-insurance policy, to an ongoing affair, to Amy's diary entries detailing an emotionally abusive and, on rare occasions, violent Nick – but is he actually behind his wife's disappearance?

SUMMARY

THE DAY OF

Nick Dunne wakes early on the morning of his fifth wedding anniversary. Despite a sense of foreboding, he says to himself that "it [is] a day for doing" (p. 8).

Through a diary entry, we are shown Amy Elliot's first encounter with Nick at a party for writers. The two instantly hit it off. These diary entries occur between every chapter in Nick's perspective, and essentially provide a counterpoint to Nick's internal narration and the image he projects.

Nick returns home from working at a bar he co-owns with his twin sister Margot, and finds signs of a struggle — but does not find Amy. The police arrive at Nick's house, and, seeing signs of a struggle, immediately call in detectives. The detectives, Rhonda Boney and Jim Gilpin, make a casual sweep of Nick's house while asking him basic questions, to Nick's internal agitation. The interview with Boney and Gilpin continues at the police station.

Nick alerts Amy's parents to her disappearance, and is told that his own father, whom he has long attempted to distance himself from, has briefly escaped again from his retirement home. Nick stays the night at Margot's house.

THE SEARCH BEGINS

Nick, slightly hungover, attends a press conference regarding Amy's disappearance. His temper is on a shorter fuse, to the point where he must tell himself: "Do not antagonize the cops" (p. 80). At the press conference, he meets his sister as well as Amy's parents, Rand and Marybeth Elliott. Nick is utterly disoriented, and fumbles the conference. He reflexively does what he always does "to remind people [he] wasn't a dick": he flashes "a killer smile" (p. 87).

The detectives allow Nick to open Amy's anniversary gift: the first clue to her usual anniversary scavenger hunts. It leads to the college where Nick works as an adjunct professor, and the second clue's accompanying love letter unsettles him. He lies to Detective Gilpin, saying he does not know what the second clue means. Later, we are shown that Nick has a disposable phone.

At the headquarters for the search for Amy, dozens begin gathering. Nick receives a tip from Stucks Buckley about the Blue Book boys, a group of homeless individuals laid off from a Blue Book factory. Search parties for Amy begin branching through the town. Nick is approached by a searcher named Shawna, who seems to be "trying to get an ego stroke from the husband of a missing woman" (p. 132), and whom he viscerally dislikes and wants to go away due to her attractiveness and the attention it brings.

AMY'S GOT A GUN

Nick arranges to go with some locals and Amy's father to the abandoned mall at night to question the homeless there, dissatisfied with the detectives' work. At night, Nick and his inquisitors go to the mall, armed with baseball bats. The group ask the homeless there if they knew anything about Amy, and when Nick shows a picture of her, a man named Lonnie says she had come there to buy a gun.

Rand and Nick ponder who would have scared Amy into thinking she needed a gun. The detectives ask questions of Nick that make it implicitly clear that he is increasingly being viewed as a viable suspect, especially when they note that he had not told them of an argument that he had with Amy the day before the disappearance.

Back at the search HQ, Nick's anger at Shawna grows. He later follows Amy's newest clue to his father's old house, where he discovers that she has changed the alarm code. Once he calls the alarm company and finally sorts out the issue, he finds the next clue — one he finally does not know. That night, at Margot's house, he receives a text on his disposable phone saying that someone is outside his door. It is Nick's mistress, Andie, a student of his whom he has been seeing for over a year. Andie insists that Nick at least call her for a few seconds every day, despite the potentially criminal danger such an affair might put him (and her) in. Margot catches Nick just after he has escorted Andie out the door early in the morning.

THE AFFAIR AND COMING HOME

Margot reprimands Nick for his affair, in particular for how bad it looks in the current situation. He finally returns home, the crime scene analysis complete. Margot tells him a highly negative television programme, Ellen Abbott, is on about him. Shawna, the woman he had rebuffed at the search headquarters, is interviewed, and she tells the titular host that Nick came off to her as flirtatious.

Nick visits Desi Collings, Amy's high school boyfriend and potential stalker. Nick attempts to probe for anything that might indicate his awareness of Amy's whereabouts, but shortly after arriving, Desi's mother requests that he leave and ask questions again only through their lawyer.

Gilpin and Boney arrange a meeting with Nick at his house. They begin interviewing Nick in more depth, and a number of alarming facts come to the surface. Not only did he have no alibi the day of Amy's disappearance, a friend of Amy's also said that Amy thought Nick married her for money; several hundred thousand dollars' worth of various goods had been bought through his credit card; and the crime scene looked suspiciously staged. Nick grows more flustered and frustrated, and closes the questions by saying that he needs a lawyer.

PUBLIC OPINION BEGINS TO TURN ON NICK

Nick gives a speech at a vigil for Amy, who has now been missing for a week. After his speech ends, Noelle Hawthorne, Amy's best friend in Carthage whom Nick had no idea was her friend at all, takes the microphone and demands that Nick confess what he has done to Amy, who, she claims, is pregnant.

Amy's diary details the incident where Nick's anger manifested physically. It is after this episode that she goes to purchase a gun from the homeless crowd in the mall.

Nick meets lawyer Tanner Bolt, famous for turning cases like his completely in favour of the defendant. During the meeting, Bolt more than shows his usefulness, and Nick hires him. On his way home, he realises the answer to Amy's last clue: it leads to the unused shed behind Margot's house.

AMY'S ELABORATE TRAP

Amy's diary entries stop, and the narration from her perspective switches to the first person, in which she has just left the carefully crafted 'crime scene' of her home. The diary entries, it turns out, were fabricated, along with many other details of her life. Her first few years with Nick, she confesses, were excellent – but a charade, with both of them acting like people they were not.

Nick calls Margot to her shed to reveal that it is full of all of the items bought by the credit cards in his name. At this point everything has clicked together for Nick: he realises that Amy has framed him in the most elaborate way possible. Nick realises, in retrospect, that every clue has led him to different places he has had sex with Andie at, and that Amy therefore knew of the affair. Margot and Nick attempt to parse out Amy's next potential clue, if it is indeed a clue and not merely a taunt: Punch and Judy puppets.

THE GETAWAY AND NICK'S PLAN OF ATTACK

Amy drives to the Missouri Ozarks to hide away. She began planning to frame Nick for her murder once she discovered his affair. From there, she decided that any other option would be letting

Nick off too easy. She wrote all the 2005-2012 diary entries in the time between discovering the affair and her own 'disappearance,' and she makes clear that she is proud of her fastidiousness and attention to detail.

Nick, on Tanner's advice, breaks up with Andie, though she does not take it well. Amy relaxes at a nondescript cabin, where she eagerly watches the news to see Nick's troubles unfold. We learn the final part of her plan: killing herself and making it look as if Nick had disposed of her body in the Mississippi River.

THE CASE AGAINST AMY

Nick tries to convince Tanner that Amy has framed him. Amy details how she faked a pregnancy. At her hideaway cabin, she 'befriends' another resident, a woman named Greta apparently on the run from an abusive significant other.

Tanner believes Nick's story about Amy's attempt to frame him, but the trio — Nick, Margot and Tanner — are backed into a corner, as they have no evidence of Amy's deviousness and Margot is now implicated by the shed full of goods. Nick calls Tommy O'Hara, a man Amy had accused of rape before dropping the charges. Tommy tells Nick how he and Amy had been dating for a while and, similarly to her relationship with Nick, the two had slowly become distant. Tommy then began showing interest in another woman. Then came the accusation, complete with incriminating evidence. Later, she dropped the charges, and Tommy received an anonymous note saying that she hoped he learned his lesson.

Amy has decided against killing herself, thinking the act unjust. Although she is initially friendly towards her cabin-mates Greta and Jeff, she begins to think they are aware of who she is, or at least might be planning to rob her. She regrets that she had any trust to give.

Nick calls Hilary Handy, a woman who allegedly stalked Amy in high school. Like with Tommy, Hilary, once given a chance to tell her story, tells Nick how Amy grew jealous of her and spent several months setting her up before throwing herself down a flight of stairs and accusing Hilary of the deed. Afterward, Nick goes to a bar, where he meets a reporter who actually roots for him: he agrees to an impromptu interview while somewhat drunk.

NICK RECOUPING PUBLIC OPINION

Amy watches Nick's interview, only to bristle at the small media success it brings him. She has also decided that it is time she left. As she clears the cabin of any traces of herself or her DNA, however, Jeff and Greta come and rob her of all her savings, having recognised that she is at least unable to safely call the police.

Tanner berates Nick for his interview stunt, but derives another idea from it: a prime-time TV interview, very carefully practiced. Nick, Margot and Tanner go to Tanner's St Louis penthouse to meet Tanner's wife Betsy, a former TV news anchor and now a lawyer like her husband, to prepare for it.

Amy calls for Desi Collings to help her in her moneyless state, and convinces him that Nick was dangerously abusive. Nick, although prepared to reveal his affair in the interview, is beaten to the punch: Andie makes her statement first. Despite this, Nick's interview is received rather well.

EVIDENCE RISES AGAINST NICK, AMY HIDES AT DESI'S

The police have acquired a warrant to search Margot's shed. They place Margot and Nick under arrest, and begin interrogating Nick. Two new key pieces of information are revealed to Nick and Tanner: that Nick's fingerprints are all over the goods in the shed, and that Amy's diary has been found.

Amy settles in Desi's lakeside mansion, which he has prepped for her arrival to a suspiciously elaborate degree despite their contact only beginning 24 hours earlier. Amy wonders whether she has made a mistake coming to him.

Gilpin and Boney interrogate Nick, and he and Tanner lay out the theory that Amy has framed him. The detectives remain unconvinced. Inwardly, Nick becomes more and more infuriated at Amy.

Amy watches Nick's interview, and upon seeing him publicly taking the blame for the severe stalls in their marriage, she begins to wonder if he has learned his lesson. Amy starts to yearn for the earlier stages of their marriage and thinks "[she] need[s] to get home to him" (p. 472).

Nick seems to recognise Amy's need to win, as he intuitively guesses that his public humiliation might draw her back. After details about the contents of Margot's shed are leaked to the media, the public begins to hate him again. Nick begins to fantasise about actually killing Amy.

NICK'S ARREST, AND AMY'S SECOND GETAWAY

Amy feels more and more trapped by Desi, who appears to be grooming her as she spends more time hiding at his lakehouse. Although she initially thought she could control him, she now realises she cannot, and "feel[s] like something very bad is going to happen" (p. 484), continuing to pine for 'New Nick'.

Nick is arrested, the police having purportedly found the 'murder weapon' on the bank of the Mississippi River. While he is home on bond and awaiting trial, Amy suddenly returns, bloodied and dishevelled. She crafts a story which pins all the blame on Desi and paints him as a maniacal stalker whom she eventually managed to kill in self-defence and escape from after watching her husband be implicated by so-called coincidences and police ineptitude. She waves off the darker parts of her diary as her having a "dramatic streak" (p. 507), though she says that the bulk of the marriage issues it traces are true.

THE RETURN

Amy returns home. She acts as if the story that she has told the police is true, but when she has Nick alone and stripped down — to make sure he is not wearing any recording devices — she tells him everything, threatening to frame him for attempted murder were he to try to leave her. Nick calls Tanner afterward to tell him how Amy confessed everything to him, but Tanner can see no way to implicate her in any part of the story given how airtight it is. His only legal advice: "Play nice" (p. 524). Nick fantasises again about actually killing Amy.

Nick attempts to convince Amy to divorce him, to no avail. He says he will file for divorce if she does not, though she threatens to devote her life to making his miserable if he does so. The two get in a heated argument, and Nick turns violent. Then, he realises that everything she said about him — that he could not live without her because no other woman could match the things she has done — was true. So instead of killing her, he decides to formulate his own plan, to trap her in her own madness or get her locked in prison.

'PLAYING NICE'

Nick and Amy spend the next several weeks pretending to be the married couple they once were. Nick works with Margot and Boney to try to craft a case against Amy, but they struggle to do so. Amy secures a book deal to tell her story; Nick himself begins writing his own book, thinking that he will merely let it play in the court of public opinion. When he is about to triumphantly show her the completed tell-all book, she drops her own bombshell: she is pregnant, and for real this time. Nick, because he wants to protect his son from his wife, agrees to drop his investigation with Boney, delete his book, and accept the blame for the shed full of credit card-bought goods.

CHARACTER STUDY

NICK DUNNE

Nick is a stereotypically handsome man – so aware of his looks and how people assume him to be a bad guy because of them, that he smiles automatically (and thus in inappropriate situations) in order to offset these assumptions.

Nick, while not guilty of his wife's disappearance or murder, exhibits many signs of guilt. His smiles in inappropriate situations are one. He has also internalised his father's misogyny, though he is aware of it and fights it constantly. He was very frustrated and distant in his marriage, struggling with feelings of inadequacy. His affair with Andie Hardy was one way to combat those feelings.

Nick, while somewhat easily flustered, is smart. His brilliance, though, only seems to shine through in his co-dependence on Amy, who herself notes that only together do the two bring out their best (and, ironically, their most toxic) aspects.

AMY ELLIOTT DUNNE

Amy is, like Nick, stereotypically beautiful. She uses this and her in-depth knowledge of her husband to manipulate public opinion against him.

Amy is extremely meticulous and competitive. She spent over a year creating a narrative in which to frame Nick for murder, and we see through Hilary Handy, Tommy O'Hara, and other smaller stories about her that Nick recounts that these traits combine dangerously with a vindictive streak.

Amy does not necessarily hate Nick, but what Nick did to her. The two show that they are codependent, so when one falters, so does the other. In order to recoup the glory days of the early years of their relationship, Amy traps Nick with the threat of a conviction for attempted murder, and then with a child. These plans evolved from her staged disappearance, which she initially used as a way to punish Nick; however, when she saw, or thought she saw, actual contrition from him, she thinks him punished enough to return to, though is prepared to keep him on a short leash.

Amy goes against many female archetypes. Instead of utilising her brilliance and attention to detail to positive effect, as many writers do today in order to write against the predominance of stereotypically masculine-dependent female characters in earlier fiction, Flynn has twisted those traits with a dash of sociopathy and self-importance. Doing so implodes the traditional narrative of femininity: not only can women be strong, they can now be maliciously dangerous.

DETECTIVE RHONDA BONEY

Boney becomes the target of many of Nick's frustrations early in the novel, when he thinks her to be doing her job poorly. She tries to help him where she can, but cannot help following where the evidence leads. She faces intense scrutiny when Amy is found, and tries to help create a case against her, but whether doing so was entirely for Nick or for her career remained uncertain.

RAND AND MARYBETH ELLIOTT

Rand and Marybeth are Amy's parents, and have degrees in psychology, like Amy. They wrote a children's book series based on their daughter called *Amazing Amy*. Amy cares little for them, and is particularly irked by their indirect analysis and financial exploitation of her through their book series. Amy thinks they deserved the stress of her disappearance.

MARGOT DUNNE

Margot is Nick's most steadfast companion, despite harbouring some doubts when certain pieces of evidence arise. She co-owns a bar in Carthage with Nick, where they started to work when their mother's cancer worsened. Her relationship with Amy was already on shaky ground even before Nick realised that Amy had framed him.

TANNER BOLT

Tanner is Nick's lawyer, and while he says he believes Nick was framed, Nick does not seem to think he is telling the truth until Amy's return. Tanner helps reclaim Nick's public image, and while Nick does not always heed his advice, what he says does seem to turn out to be Nick's best option.

Tanner rose to prominence as a lawyer for taking cases just like Nick's and turning them around: cases where husbands appear fully implicated in a crime. As such, he is renowned, but also known as the one people call when they are guilty.

DESI COLLINGS

Desi once dated Amy in high school, and has a strange obsession with her still. The obsession seems to stem from his own mother, whom Nick recognises as looking exactly like an older version of Amy.

Desi, while not abusive in the way Amy paints Nick as in her fake diaries, still exhibits his own form of toxic masculinity when Amy hides at his lakehouse. He constantly mentions that he has helped her, frequently touches her, and thrives on being considered a 'white knight'; combined with a tall gate at his house and giving Amy no passcode to get out of it and no money, Amy rightfully feels trapped by him.

ANDIE HARDY

Andie began having an affair with Nick over a year before Amy's disappearance. A student at the college where Nick works as an adjunct journalism professor, Andie is young and attractive, but, as Amy herself points out, simple compared to Amy, who brings out the best Nick can be. Amy knows that Nick would not be satisfied with Andie in the long run.

HILARY HANDY AND TOMMY O'HARA

Hilary and Tommy provide counter-narratives to the image Amy has created for herself of the perfect and widely-loved wife. The two have histories similar to Nick's new one: they befriended Amy, then crossed her (sometimes, in Hilary's case, in seemingly insignificant ways), and Amy enacted a complex and destructive revenge against them. Their stories, however, are not seen as useful for Nick: they both have additional histories with substance abuse and legal issues.

ANALYSIS

MANIPULATION OF EVIDENCE: THE PUBLIC, THE MEDIA, AND PERCEPTION

Gone Girl shows that fabricating a plausible narrative to cover your tracks is not necessarily easy, but possible. Amy, over the course of the planning and enactment of her plan, makes her mantra one of patience, noting how many murderers and other criminals do not get away with the crime simply because they decided against patient and meticulous planning. With her plan, she manages to abuse two things: the media and the public. These two entities, in contrast to her meticulous nature, live on eye-catching headlines and instant gratification. As Tanner notes, once a case becomes public enough, the jury pool for the actual legal trial likely becomes tainted; as such, Amy successfully manoeuvres the media and public's fickle and short-sighted nature as a massive weight against Nick.

What is implied in this is that it is not the story itself that matters, but how it is presented. Nick's persona vacillates in the public eye between loving husband and abusive cheater as quickly as the evidence for either surfaces. Amy attempts to guide this hair-trigger entity, as do Tanner and Nick himself: as even Amy's perspective shows, even the most meticulous of planning can sometimes have trouble guiding events in the desired direction.

It is important to note the distinction between the private life of the individuals involved, and the public as an entity. The lives of the Dunnes and the Elliotts, as well as other smaller actors in the unfolding story of Nick and Amy's marriage, become intimate and clear to the reader since we get in-depth looks at their perspectives and the consequences of Amy's disappearance and return (a rather ironic analysis, considering the analysis of the public to follow). They have little control over public perception of their plights, even though that public perception essentially shows how difficult their lives will be for any particular day. In contrast, the public is not shown, except en masse: a crowd of reporters or protesters, a vigil, anonymous online comments. Characters such as Shawna Kelly and Noelle Hawthorne only remain in Nick's orbit long enough to gather a superficial amount of information on him and then unload it in the public eye, and even seemingly well-meaning reporters such as Sharon Schieber and Rebecca ultimately do what they do for their job rather than Nick's unabridged story.

In effect, the public exhibits a mob mentality. Details have to be watered down, simplified, in order for Nick or anyone else to have any say in how they are perceived. Despite the public having so much control over the reception of Nick's story, the public ultimately 'already knows' what has happened: it merely wants its biases played out in real time for entertainment purposes.

LEVERAGING STEREOTYPICAL GENDER ROLES

To this blinded public, Amy is perfection: a loving, pregnant wife attempting to win back her dangerously abusive husband, and beautiful as well. As such, in tandem with her disappearance, she is universally loved by the public – barring outliers such as Hilary Handy and Tommy O'Hara – but Nick (and the reader) knows that this is a carefully constructed persona designed to elicit just such a universal love.

Amy leverages this persona against Nick through the public, which, due to shows such as *Ellen Abbott*, has accepted a rather singular idea of femininity. Women – particularly beautiful women – are inherently nurturing, fragile, loving, and so on, or so the public likes to believe. Amy's public persona confirms all these biases, and so makes it easier for the public reaction to flurry in her favour.

Misogyny itself is a major theme of the novel. These ideas regarding femininity are damaging – not only because it allows for someone like Amy to leverage them, but because it makes it seem that women inherently need to depend on a male figure (as Desi Collings seems to believe, or wants to believe) – and these are not the only female stereotypes the novel deals with. Nick and his father – much more so his father – are, at their core, misogynists. Nick's father externalises his misogyny so that it is quite obvious as he spews gendered slurs, but Nick himself also has little patience for women, a fact he is aware of and attempts to subdue. The misogyny exhibited by both father and son generally manifests in a belief that women constantly nag or otherwise get in the way of masculine desires. Women, for these two, are obstacles in the way of masculine achievement.

Amy leverages these masculine misogynies as well. As public opinion confirms its biases in Amy, it is also confirmed in Nick's public portrayal: for the public, it is always the husband at fault or who is guilty in situations of spousal disappearance or murder. Social ideas of masculinity could include independence, pursuit of goals, sexual appetite, anger – all traits that Nick himself has, and which the public jumps on.

THE FAKE PERSONA

It has been noted that Amy constructed multiple personalities to win over the public. Amy, however, is not the only person to do so. Nick himself has Betsy Bolt, Tanner Bolt's wife, assist in changing his appearance and demeanour in order to appear more palatable for the public, and he and Amy, when Amy returns, pretend at being a loving family once again while internally they are essentially waging domestic war. Rand and Marybeth Elliott seem to be great parents, but Amy's diary and then Amy's first-person perspective show them to be strangely passive-aggressive in writing their *Amazing Amy* books to detail a more ideal daughter. Furthermore, Andie Hardy, Nick's mistress, appears to have radically different personas in private, on social media, and in the public.

Other such examples exist in the novel, to the point where, if one were to look closely enough, almost every character could be seen as projecting a persona that does not reflect their true selves – perhaps the one exception is the group of homeless people at Carthage's abandoned mall, who have no real public image left to lose.

Gone Girl, then, shows that we change personas based on the situation we are in. This is perhaps not a revelatory understanding for many; the novel, however, pushes that persona-change to such extremes that it truly examines its social use. In many ways it can act as an aegis for those in trouble they do not deserve – Nick and Andie, for example – but in others it can deflect from or hide toxic personality traits – as seen in the character of Amy. From this, we see that personal presentation changes from a reflection of who someone is, to something that can simply be used: personality is no longer real, it is merely a social tool.

FURTHER REFLECTION

SOME QUESTIONS TO THINK ABOUT...

- Amy's character has been simultaneously decried as anti-feminist for playing up female stereotypes in order to set her own malign plans in motion, and praised as feminist for playing a role – the out-and-out sociopathic villain – not often played by female characters. Which of these viewpoints do you agree with most? Is there some middle ground?
- How does *Gone Girl* utilise archetypes and stereotypes of feminine and masculine behaviour in order to manipulate reader response?
- How does *Gone Girl* show the implications of public opinion in issues of legality? Think in particular within the context of television and the internet.
- *Gone Girl* constantly withholds details. What is the importance of considering a story in its entirety, as opposed to understanding and responding to a story as it unfolds?

- Nick and the media have a strained relationship – ironically, given his background as a journalist. In what ways does *Gone Girl* explore the impact of the media and the public on individuals and families? In particular, how does this impact manifest once the media and the public lose interest in the story?
- What are some of the ethical issues related to media and public interest in, circulation of, and participation in cases like Nick's?
- What are some examples of less prominent forms of misogyny in the novel – that is, misogyny that does not involve slurs or outright violence?
- How does *Gone Girl* treat the relationship between parents and their children? In particular, consider the relationship between Amy and her parents, and Nick and his parents, as well as the unexplored relationship between Nick and Amy and their own child.
- In what ways does *Gone Girl* consider any individual person to be 'constructed' for social purposes (for example, Amy creates and names multiple identities for herself)? In what ways is this constructing of fake, but

socially expedient, personalities beneficial or deleterious for individuals and for the society they reside in?

We want to hear from you!
Leave a comment on your online library
and share your favourite books on social media!

FURTHER READING

REFERENCE EDITION

- Flynn, G. (2014) *Gone Girl*. New York City: Broadway Books.

ADAPTATIONS

- *Gone Girl*. (2014) [Film]. David Fincher. Dir. USA: Twentieth Century Fox, Regency Enterprises.

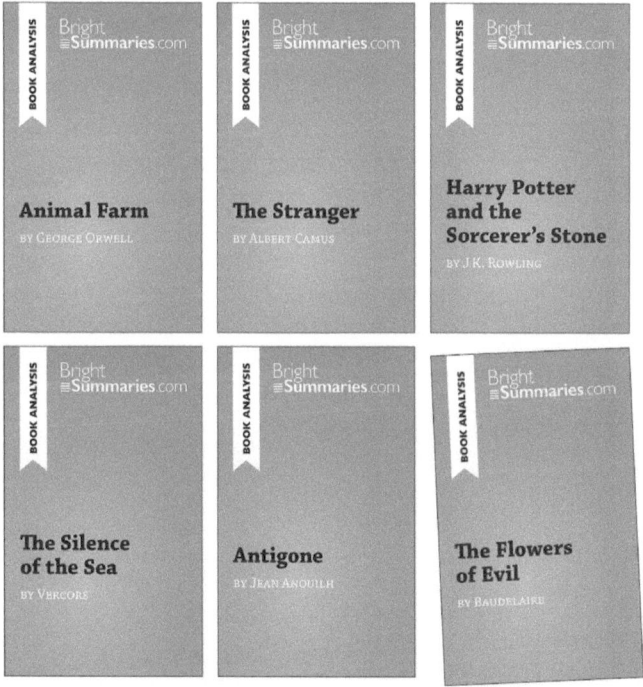

www.brightsummaries.com

Ebook EAN: 9782808017428

Paperback EAN: 9782808017435

Legal Deposit: D/2019/12603/38

Cover: © Primento

Digital conception by Primento, the digital partner of
publishers.